Real-Life Kings

Karen Latchana Kenney

LERNER PUBLICATIONS ◆ MINNEAPOLIS

Note to Educators

Throughout this book, you'll find critical-thinking questions. These can be used to engage young readers in thinking critically about the topic and in using the text and photos to do so.

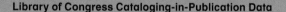

Lerner Publications Company
A division of Lerner Publishing Group, Inc.
241 First Avenue North
Minneapolis, MN 55401 USA

For reading levels and more information, look up this title at www.lernerbooks.com.

Library of Congress Cataloging-in-Publication Data

Names: Kenney, Karen Latchana, author.
Title: Real-life kings / Karen Latchana Kenney.
Description: Minneapolis : Lerner Publications, [2020] | Series: Bumba books. real-life royalty | Audience: Ages 4–7 | Audience: Grade K to Grade 3 | Includes bibliographical references and index.
Identifiers: LCCN 2018048866 (print) | LCCN 2018060373 (ebook) | ISBN 9781541561311 (eb pdf) | ISBN 9781541557307 (lb ; alk. paper) | ISBN 9781541573567 (pb ; alk. paper)
Subjects: LCSH: Kings and rulers—Juvenile literature.
Classification: LCC JC375 (ebook) | LCC JC375 .K39 2020 (print) | DDC 321.8/70922—dc23

LC record available at https://lccn.loc.gov/2018048866

Manufactured in the United States of America
1-46145-45750-3/11/2019

Table of Contents

Let's Meet a King!

King Felipe of Spain

took an oath.

He promised to serve

his people.

King Felipe

King Felipe is royalty.

His wife is the queen.

His daughters are

princesses.

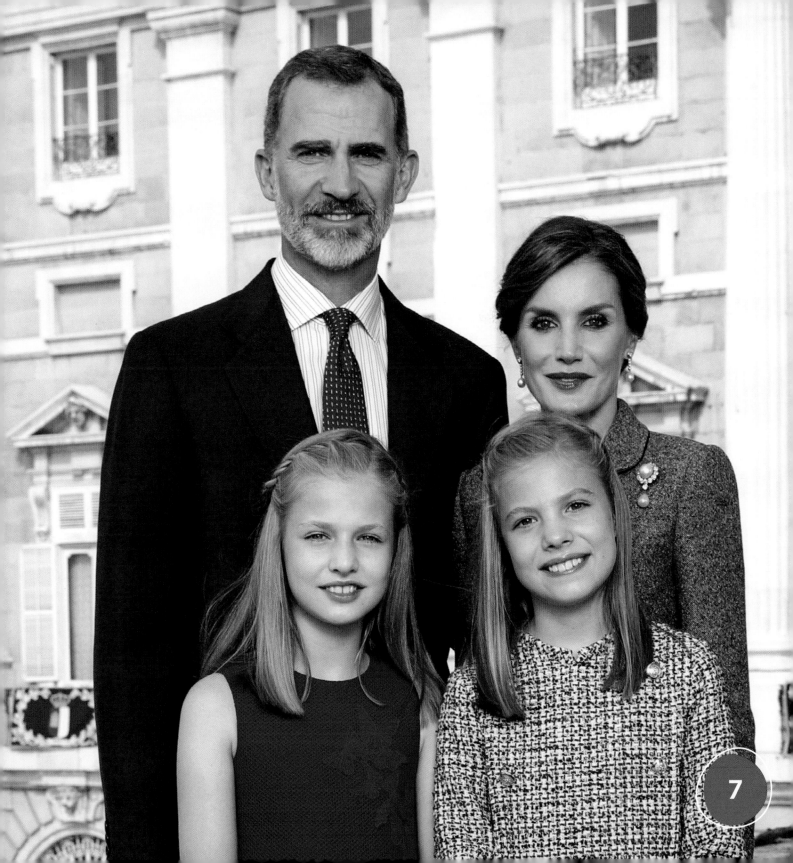

King Willem-Alexander
from the Netherlands

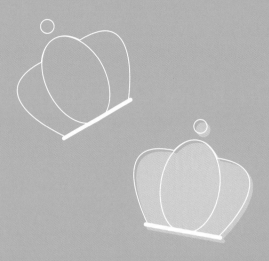

People are proud of their king.

He is a symbol of their country.

Crowds greet the king of

the Netherlands.

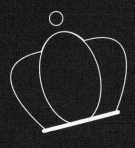

In Tonga, the king has

a crown.

Sometimes King Tupou

wears robes.

He sits on a throne.

Why do you think kings wear crowns?

King Tupou

King George from the United Kingdom

Some kings live in palaces.

The last British king, George VI,

lived at Buckingham Palace.

King Philippe of Belgium

works at a palace.

He meets with people.

He signs laws and

writes letters.

King Philippe

Many kings were once soldiers.

King Abdullah of Jordan

was in the army.

He wears his army medals.

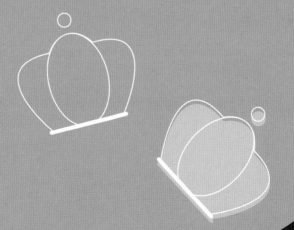

Kings meet with leaders of other countries.

They talk about their countries.

They help their countries get along.

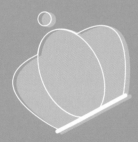

Why is it good for countries to get along?

King Harald V
from Norway

King Jigme
from Bhutan

20

A king loves his country.

He works to help his people.

Life as a King

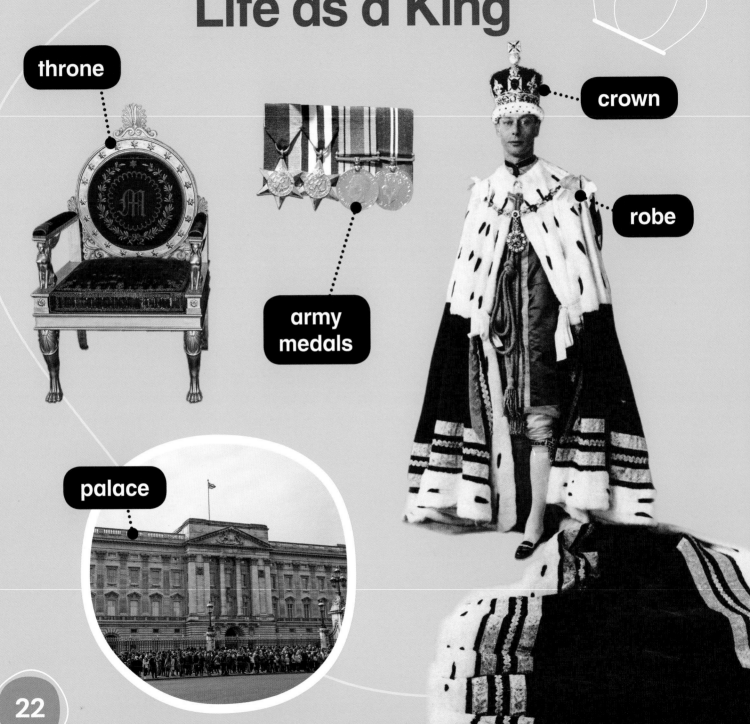

throne

crown

robe

army medals

palace

Picture Glossary

oath

a promise to do something

royalty

a person or people who belong to a royal family

symbol

something or someone that stands for something else

throne

a special chair used by a king or queen

Read More

Arnold, Tedd. *Fly Guy Presents: Castles*. New York: Scholastic, 2017.

Kenney, Karen Latchana. *Real-Life Princesses*. Minneapolis: Lerner Publications, 2020.

Kenney, Karen Latchana. *Real-Life Queens.* Minneapolis: Lerner Publications, 2020.

Index

Photo Credits

Image credits: Andreas Rentz/Getty Images, pp. 5, 23 (top left); Handout/Getty Images, pp. 6, 23 (top right); Patrick van Katwijk /Getty Images, pp. 8, 23 (bottom left); Edwina Pickles/Fairfax Media/Stringer/Getty Images, p. 11; Hulton Deutsch/Getty Images, p. 12; William Van Hecke/Getty Images, p. 15; Max Mumby/Indigo/Getty Images, p. 16; Franco Origlia/Getty Images, p. 19; Paul Bronstein/Getty Images, p. 20; LEON NEAL/Getty Images, p. 22 (medals); Jack Taylor/Stringer/Getty Images, p. 22 (palace); Universal History Archive/Getty Images, p. 22 (robes and crown); picture alliance/Getty Images, p. 22 (throne).

Cover: Paula Bronstein/Getty Images.